W9-DJK-351

JUNIOR COLLEGE DISTRICT
of St. Louis - St. Louis County
LIBRARY
5801 Wilson Ave.
St. Louis, Missouri 63110

JOSEPH FLOCH

JOSEPH FLOCH

Introductory Essays by
Julius S. Held
Jean Cassou
Laurence Schmeckebier

Thomas Yoseloff
New York • South Brunswick • London

Thomas Yoseloff, Publisher
Cranbury, New Jersey

Thomas Yoseloff, Ltd
18 Charing Cross Road
London W. C. 2, England

6423
Manufactured in the United States of America
Color Plates printed in Holland

CONTENTS

INTRODUCTION

Amidst the deafening clamor of modern art, it is a relief to encounter a painter whose work is dedicated to the noble if unfashionable proposition that art should be seen, not heard. Joseph Floch's paintings assault our acoustic sense as little as the well-brought-up child would have done in a stricter society than ours. Yet, as is the case with some of the correct children we meet in novels of Henry James, we sense a disquieting dimension below the bland surface of seemly propriety. The silence of Floch's pictures is the silence of deep waters.

The analogy, indeed, goes further; it touches the very appearance of his canvases. Though the spaces Floch paints at first seem to belong to the world of our common experience, we soon notice that they deny us the freedom of physical access. They belong to an Atlantis glimpsed tantalizingly below a still body of water or they extend into immeasurable distances behind effective barriers of invisible glass. These spaces are accentuated by walls, screens, stairs, scaffolds, and all kinds of stage paraphernalia; they are organized by virtue of light, color, and perspective. Yet they remain hushed and immobilized, even when a specific detail is given prominence by an especially concentrated light. Floch's tonal harmonies are apt to evoke the cool silvery blue of a

moonlit night rather than a hot day of summer. Above all, while everything is lucid up to a point, nothing is tangible. We see it all clearly but it remains inaccessible to our touch. In other words, Floch the artist is more of a seer than an observer; a dreamer more than a drummer; a poet, not a reporter.

Examining Floch's work from 40 years of intense activity, one is struck by its consistency. Through all the changes and variations, Floch remained faithful to an artistic credo he formulated in the very beginning of his career. Alert to the artistic manifestations of his age, he also studied — selectively, to be sure — the art that had gone before him. He never shared the contempt for tradition that has become a younger generation's passport to fame. He knew that awareness of tradition is no sign of weakness and that an artist can learn from other artists and still be himself.

Floch admits a special debt to Hans von Marées (1837-1887) who, during Floch's formative years, indeed occupied an exalted position in German art circles. Floch absorbed other influences as time went on: Dutch (Vermeer), French (Cézanne), Italian (Piero della Francesca), but he never abandoned the search for order and timeless purity that had also been Marées' deepest concern. The path Floch took later on was of necessity different. Long before he actually settled in Paris in 1925 he had become aware of the achievements of Cubism. Witness his album of lithographs, recording impressions of Palestine in the wake of a prolonged visit to the Holy Land. In Paris, the serious young Austrian was noticed by none other than Berthe Weill, who exhibited his works for six years, while he made the acquaintance of such artists as Suzanne Valadon, Utrillo, Dérain, Friesz, Gromaire, Pascin and others.

Before the war and the collapse of France forced Floch to leave Europe, he completed two large allegorical murals, originally destined for the townhall of Vincennes, but actually located in the College of Industrial Arts at Brive (Corrèze).

America provided Floch with new visual impressions and may have contributed to an intensification and refinement of his color-scale. The secret geometry of his compositions acquired a new ruggedness from the girders and pylons of the urban landscape around him. But Floch also sensed deeply the ultimate loneliness of people caught amidst the frozen mountains of steel and concrete. As he paints them, in quiet poses, they seem to listen where no one speaks to them. They seem to wait, but don't know for what.

Floch did not need figures to express isolation and unfulfilled hope. In a memorable canvas he painted a row of four chairs, each one slightly different from the next in shape and position. They, too, seem to be waiting, forlorn in space, like many of Floch's people.

Yet ultimately, Floch's art is neither gloomy nor depressing. Anyone who has seen Floch's drawings knows that whatever moves him is transformed by, and made bearable because of, an innate tenderness and tact. Though cosmopolitan, Floch still carries with him the heritage of a prior Austria, where force was fittingly suffused with gentleness, and the very sound of language was apt to take the edge off any harsh statement. Floch's drawings reveal clearly the lyrical ground of his art. His line has strength, but it is the strength of the reed, not of steel.

The drawings lay bare what may be the innermost secret of Floch's art. All his life, as I see it, he has adhered to the notion — as old as the Greeks, but as unfashionable today as the beginning statement — that the artist is a purveyor of beauty. He has given us works which are consistently beautiful, and we are in Joseph Floch's debt for never having forgotten this aspect of the artist's function.

JULIUS S. HELD
Professor of Art History
Barnard College
Columbia University

8

FOREWORD

It has been a long while since anyone has spoken of the genre of "interiors" — *peinture d'intérieur.* In fact, no one speaks nowadays of any "genre." Yet this particular type reflects one of the basic orientations of human behavior, for at bottom we are drawn either toward the exterior or the interior, and modern psychology classifies men in accordance with this line of division. In art we shall, therefore, always have "interiors."

The work of Joseph Floch belongs to this category, and can even be associated with that tradition which specialized in "interiors" — from the Dutch to Vuillard. But to the "interiors" thus cultivated by Floch must be added the entire aura of sentiments and dreams with which surrealism, aided by psychoanalysis, has enriched our concept of "interior." It is therefore with a modern eye, schooled in the poetic investigations of surrealism, that we must look at Floch's pictures. This essentially modern painter has renewed the genre and the notion of "interiors," and his art is to be ranked in the wake of Surrealism and among the most subtle poetic explorations of our day. There is something of witchcraft and enigma in the serene rooms depicted by Floch — where the disposition of a piece of furniture, the presence of a human figure, and an open door create a space singular in its effect and drenched in silence. Even the "exteriors" of Floch — views of New York, factory yards under construction, decorated with strange, enormous statues — have an air of silent mystery. Indeed, to a degree, they can also be regarded as "interiors." In short, wherever his always sensitive, vibrant, and alert curiosity carries him, Floch is a painter who never fails to take into account that imponderable which man harbors within himself and which poets call the soul — a soul that by obscure and secret communications he recognizes in everything surrounding him. Each one of these things becomes "soul" in its turn, each one "interiorizes."

It is this surrender to what is utterly intimate within him that constitutes the painting of Floch and makes of it an "interior" — an art which requires great finesse, great exactitude of touch, a very sure sense of distance and perspective, in short, an extraordinary faculty for translating into plastic signs manifold delicacies of a spiritual order. Such are the qualities demanded by the creation of an "interior" — rare and marvellous qualities. Joseph Floch, a profound artist, essentially a philosopher and a musician, possesses them. They are, in fact, the qualities which define his exceptional art.

JEAN CASSOU
Conservateur en Chef
Museum of Modern Art, Paris

9

JOSEPH FLOCH IN 1966

"Art is mankind's memory," Joseph Floch was quoted as saying in *American Artist*, for February, 1949. "How deeply touched I was to see the paintings of Van Gogh derived from Rembrandt and Delacroix! The spirit of one painter flows over into the spirit of another." The manifestos of rebellion issued by artists during the past two generations have not crushed the quiet voice of historical conscience of the dedicated contemporary who has been able to support his convictions through a long and sustained artistic performance.

A native of Vienna, Austria, he was educated at the Vienna Academy of Fine Arts during the later years of the first World War and developed in the poetic color tradition of the impressionists and the newly organized *Hagenbund*, a society of progressive artists of which he was one of the founders (1919).

At that time he travelled to Munich and encountered for the first time the Great French Masters of the 19th Century, especially Manet as well as Cézanne and the great Hans von Marées. In 1921 he lived and worked in Holland under the influence of Rembrandt, Seghers, Vermeer and the spacious atmosphere of this country. A trip to Palestine result-ed in many drawings and paintings as well as a portfolio of lithographs *Palestine*, published by Harz in Berlin and acquired by the Albertina Museum in Vienna. In 1925 he settled in Paris where he was associated with Berthe Weill's famous gallery on the rue Laffitte whose protegés included such distinguished early modern painters as Pascin, Suzanne Valadon, Vlaminck, Utrillo, Gromaire and other leading artists.

His first opportunity to exhibit in Paris was at the Salon d'Automne and the Salon des Tuilleries in 1926. His first one-man show there was held at Berthe Weill's in 1929. These met with immediate success and through the ensuing years he continued to participate in the major international exhibitions of both Europe and America. Honors and awards include the gold medal at the Paris International in 1937, commissions from the French government for murals in the Ecole Supérieure Industrielle in Brive (Corrèze) in 1939, the Lippincott at the Pennsylvania Academy of Fine Arts in 1944, the National Academy of Arts and Letters award of 1951, the Brevoort Eikemeier Prize from Columbia University in 1955, the Isidor Memorial Gold Medal of the National Academy, the William Palmer Memorial

Prize in 1960 and many others. In 1962 he was made Chevalier of the French Order of Arts and Letters.

His work has been included in the permanent collection of the Museum of Modern Art in Paris, the Museum of the City of Paris, the Jeu de Paume, the Albertina and the Belvedeer Museum of Vienna, the Museums of Grenoble and Lille, the Tel Aviv and Jerusalem Museums as well as the Metropolitan and the Whitney Museums of New York, the De Young Museum in San Francisco, the Toledo Museum, the William Rockhill Nelson Gallery in Kansas City and many other American and European Museums.

From the beginning, critics recognized in his work something which was characteristic of our time but also a special quality that belonged to the great tradition. His was a classic conception, his Austrian compatriot Hans Tietze wrote in 1928, which was rooted in the rich cultural environment of Old Vienna, but was nourished by the inspiring and luminous atmosphere of contemporary Paris. Waldemar George, in the *Prisme des Arts* (1958, No. 15) associated Floch with the *Paysage Humaniste*, with its ideal of man in his natural environment.

The recent world war brought dramatic changes, and in July, 1941, he emigrated with his wife and two small daughters to the United States and took permanent residence in New York City. "I was overwhelmed by the enormous sight," he wrote, and it took me several years to re-evoke architectural space in painting and to find the real expression of this new world." In 1952, the venerable Henry McBride, in the *Art News*, was impressed by this artist who composes with "an infallible sense of design and his colors, though somber, are rich" — a pure painter with no tricks, no virtuosity and no literary content.

From 1942 on he has had a continuous record of one man shows at the Associated American Artists and more recently at the Forum Gallery in New York, and has participated in nearly all the significant national exhibitions such as the Whitney, the Cocoran, the Carnegie International, those of the Chicago Institute, the Pennsylvania Academy and many others. A number of significant one-man shows have been held in the Toledo, Ohio, Museum of Art, the De Young Museum in San Francisco, and that of Syracuse University.

This long record of personal achievement and public recognition is worth studying, especially for those of us who are commited to the education of young artists as well as their patrons. Too often we seem caught in the hysteria of devotion to the Old Masters as aesthetic supermen and an equally blind involvement in the rapid succession and obsolescence of contemporary artistic styles. The recent and magnificent retrospective exhibition of his work held at Syracuse University in December, 1965 was a monument to the personal achievement of this man who painted as he pleased with ever increasing clarity and power. In our constant search for the new and the venturous we among the historians, educators and critics do well to consider the integration of the present with the past in our inevitable drive toward the future, and to honor our contemporary masters.

LAURENCE SCHMECKEBIER, Dean
The School of Art
Syracuse University

JOSEPH FLOCH – A CHRONOLOGY

1895 November 5, born in Vienna, Austria.

1913 Graduated from high school (Realschule).

1913-1918 Entered Academy of Fine Arts, Vienna, Austria, and attended Master School under Rudolf Bacher and Franz Rumpler.

1919 Co-founder of *Hagenbund*, a society of the foremost young Avant-Garde artists in Vienna.

1923 First one-man show in Vienna. Wandered six months through Palestine. Albertina Museum, Vienna acquired drawings and a portfolio *Palestine* (ten lithographs with an introduction by E. Conrat Tietze.) Exhibited in many international group-shows. From this time yearly exhibitions in Vienna until 1925.

1924 *Die Graphische Künste* (*Graphic Arts*) published a special issue by Max Eisler about his work.

1925 Settled in Paris.

1927 Honorable mention at International Exhibition in Bordeaux.

1928 Important articles by Professor Hans Tietze in *Deutsche Kunst und Dekoration*. Many other articles in various art magazines.

1929 First one-man show at gallery Berthe Weill, Paris, (preface of catalogue by Jean Richard Bloch) followed by several one-man shows during the period ending in 1933 in the same gallery.

1931 One-man show, Philadelphia, Crillon Gallery, of forty paintings. Commission by Louis Jouvet for the sets of Jean Giraudoux's play, *Judith*. (Theatre Pigalle, Paris)

1932 Critical and biographical articles in leading art magazines by Jacques Guenne, Paul Fierens, Waldemar George, André Salmon, Hans Tietze and others.

1933 One-man show: Pierre Colle Gallery, Paris. Retrospective show: Hagenbund, Vienna.

1933-1936 One-man shows: Reinhardt Museum, Winterthur, Switzerland, and Goudstikker Gallery, Amsterdam, Holland. Ten paintings in exhibition of Contemporary Masters, Antwerp Museum, Belgium, organized by Jeu de Paume Museum, Paris).

1934 May 12, married Hermine Fränkl.

1935 March 1, daughter, Jenny Eva, born.

1936 One-man show: Gallery Jeanne Castel, Paris. Jeu de Paume Museum, Paris, purchased two paintings. Important articles by Jean Cassou (*Art et Decoration*) and by Waldemar George (*Formes*).

1937 Exhibited at International exhibition of paintings, Paris. (Gold medal)

1938 French Government purchased two paintings and commissioned two murals.

1939 June 4, daughter, Suzanne Marguerite, born. Exhibited at World's Fair, New York.

1940 One-man show: Gallery Jouvène, Marseille.

1941 Settled in New York.
One-man show: Toledo Art Museum, Toledo, Ohio. The museum acquired one painting.

1942 One-man show: AAA Gallery (Associated American Artists) New York. One-man shows in this gallery continued until 1956. Article by R. Frost in *Art News*.
From this date on, participated regularly in exhibitions at numerous museums, including Carnegie (Pittsburgh), Whitney (New York), Corcoran (Washington, D.C.), Pennsylvania Academy (Philadelphia).
Encyclopedia Britannica acquired one painting.

1945 Received Lippincott Prize, The Pennsylvania Academy of Fine Arts.

1946 French Government acquired two paintings for Museum of Modern Art, Paris.

1947 Received purchase Prize, Museum of Fine Arts, Springfield, Mass.
Article by Georges Huisman in *Arts*, Paris.

1951 Became American Citizen
Received award of the National Institute of Arts and Letters.

1952 Maximilien Gautier published book: *Joseph Floch*, Editions Gemaux, Paris.
Article by Henry McBride, *Art News* New York.

1955 One-man show: De Young Memorial Museum, San Francisco.

Bezalel Museum, Jerusalem acquired one painting.
Received from Columbia University the Brevoort-Eickemeyer Prize.
Retrospective article (by Erica Tietze Conrat) in a special issue *Die Kunst*, Munich.

1956 One-man show: Gallery Drouant-David, Paris.
Belvedere Museum, Vienna, acquired two paintings.
Museum of Modern Art, Paris, and Museum of the City of Paris acquired paintings.

1958 One-man show: ACA Gallery, New York. Paintings acquired by the Metropolitan Museum of Art (Hugo Kastor fund), the Whitney Museum of American Art, and the Museum of Tel Aviv, Israel. (American-Israel Cultural Foundation.)

1960 Received Edwin Palmer Memorial Prize, N. A., New York

1961 Joined Forum Gallery, New York.

1962 Appointed faculty member of the New School for Social Research.

1963 Nominated Chevalier of the French Order of Arts and Letters. (First American artist to receive this distinction.)
Received Joseph S. Isidor Gold Medal, N. A., New York.

1964 One-man show: Forum Gallery, New York.
Received Adolph and Clara Obrig Prize, N. A., New York.

1965 One-man show: Museum of Syracuse University, Syracuse, New York.

1966 Received first prize Eastern States Exhibition, Museum of Fine Arts, Springfield, Mass.

1967 Received Saltus Gold Medal of Merit, N. A., New York.

COLOR PLATES

(Listed in Chronological Order)

ON THE TERRACE, 1950, *Collection of the Artist*

STILL LIFE WITH BLUE BOTTLE, 1959, *Collection of the Artist*

THE STUDIO, 1960, *Collection of Mr. Meyer Zinn, New York*

THE NEW WORLD, 1960, *Collection of the Artist*

CITY NEAR THE SEA, 1962, *Collection of Dr. and Mrs. Hindels*

REST, 1962, *Metropolitan Museum, New York*

DUNES, 1963, *Collection of Mr. and Mrs. Otto Manley*

YOUNG WOMEN, 1964, *Collection of the Artist*

DOG ON TERRACE, 1964, *Private Collection*

STANDING NUDE, 1964, *Collection of the Artist*

THE ISLAND, 1964, *Collection of the Artist*

REST, 1965, *Collection of the Artist*

MONOCHROME PLATES

(C—Collection of. CA—Collection of the Artist)

1 SELF PORTRAIT, 1964, C Mr. and Mrs. Herbert A. Goldstone

2 LUNZERSEE, 1922, C Dr. and Mrs. B. Lowenfeld, Berkeley, Cal.

3 WOMEN ON THE BEACH, 1924, former C of Helena Rubinstein, Paris.

4 CHILDREN, DRAWING, 1915. C Mr. Raphael Soyer,

5 AROUND THE TABLE, 1927, C Mr. and Mrs. Eric Cohn, N. Y.

6 JOSE MARIA VALERA, 1926, CA.

7 BIRD, 1927, CA.

8 BATHERS, 1928, CA.

9 HEAD OF A WOMAN, 1926, C A. Tietze, Los Angeles, Cal.

10 DOGS ON A TERRACE, 1928, Private Collection.

11 ON THE BEACH, 1928, C Chana Orloff, Paris.

12 AGAVAS, 1927, C Dr. Frederick Fraenkl, New York.

13 RIDER, DRAWING, 1923, private collection.

14 BATHERS ON THE BEACH, 1928, private collection.

15 ON LAKE TIBERIAS, LITHOGRAPH, 1923, Albertina Museum, Vienna, Austria.

16 MAN AND DOG, 1928, CA.

17 THE ROAD, 1929, C Mrs. Dorothy Oko, New York.

18 EVENING, 1928, C Mrs. Frederick Knize, New York.

19 DRAWING, 1928.

20 SPANISH LANDSCAPE, 1929, C Dr. and Mrs. Arthur Grishman, New York.

21 THE MODELS, 1935, C Dr. Helen Deutsch, Cambridge, Mass.

22 MY MOTHER, DRAWING, 1929, CA.

23 SICILIAN LANDSCAPE, 1930, C Mrs. Helen R. Veltford, Palo Alto, Cal.

24 INTERIEUR D'ÉTÉ, 1933, Abbot Museum.

25 TAPESTRY, 1938, private collection.

26 CONVERSATION 1, 1937, C Dr. E. Oberholzer, Jr., New York.

27 VIEW FROM A WINDOW, 1936, C Mrs. A. Luchsinger, Zurich, Switzerland.

28 TERRACE WITH ROCK, 1938, CA.

29 WOMAN SEATED, 1937, Museum of Fine Arts, Toledo, Ohio.

30 TERASSE ANIMÉE, 1935, C Miss Peggy Passavant, New York.

31 ROCKY LANDSCAPE, WASHDRAWING, 1936, CA.

32 SILENT ROOM, 1937, CA.

33 BRIDGE, 1944, CA.

34 MANHATTAN ROOFS, Museum of Modern Art, Paris.

35 PENTHOUSE TERRACE, 1943, C Dr. Frederick Fraenkl, New York.

36 ROOFTOP IN MANHATTAN, 1943, CA.

37 CONSTRUCTION, 1951, C Arbis Blatas, New York.

38 MATERNITY 1952, DRAWING.

39 WOMAN, 1961, DRAWING.

40 INTERIOR WITH BLACK SCREEN, 1946, C Dr. and Mrs. G. Bychowski, New York.

41 SISTERS, 1950, Museum of Modern Art, Paris.

42 FISHERMAN, 1948, De Young Museum, San Francisco, Cal.

43 STAIRWAY, private collection.

44 BROODING WOMAN, 1950, CA.

45 BROWN SCREEN, 1942, CA.

46 STUDIO WITH SEASHELL, 1950, Museum of Lille, France.

47 GIRL, DRAWING, C Mr. and Mrs. Raphael Soyer, New York, 1950.

48 VIEW IN SAN FRANCISCO, 1953, C Mr. and Mrs. H. Popper, San Francisco, Cal.

49 MATERNITY, 1948, Museum of Fine Arts, Springfield, Mass.

50 HEAD, 1947, CA.

51 WATERING THE FLOWERS, 1952, CA.

PLATES

1 SELF PORTRAIT

2 LUNZERSEE

3 WOMEN ON THE BEACH

4 Children

5 AROUND THE TABLE

7 BIRD

8 BATHERS

9 HEAD OF A WOMAN

10 Dogs on a Terrace

11 ON THE BEACH

12 Agavas

13 RIDER

14 Bathers on the Beach

STILL LIFE WITH BLUE BOTTLE

CITY NEAR THE SEA

15 ON LAKE TIBERIAS

16 MAN AND DOG

17 THE ROAD

18 EVENING

ICI • 314 • 71YR 08/119 • ICI
ICI • 314 • 71YR 08/119 • ICI
ICI • 314 • 71YR 08/119 • ICI

ICI • 314 • 71YR 08/119 • ICI
ICI • 314 • 71YR 08/119 • ICI
ICI • 314 • 71YR 08/119 • ICI
ICI • 314 • 71YR 08/119 • ICI
ICI • 314 • 71YR 08/119 • ICI
ICI • 314 • 71YR 08/119 • ICI
ICI • 314 • 71YR 08/119 • ICI
ICI • 314 • 71YR 08/119 • ICI
ICI • 314 • 71YR 08/119 • ICI
ICI • 314 • 71YR 08/119 • ICI
ICI • 314 • 71YR 08/119 • ICI
ICI • 314 • 71YR 08/119 • ICI
ICI • 314 • 71YR 08/119 • ICI

19 Drawing

20 Spanish Landscape

21 THE MODELS

22 MY MOTHER

23 Sicilian Landscape

24 Interieur d'Été

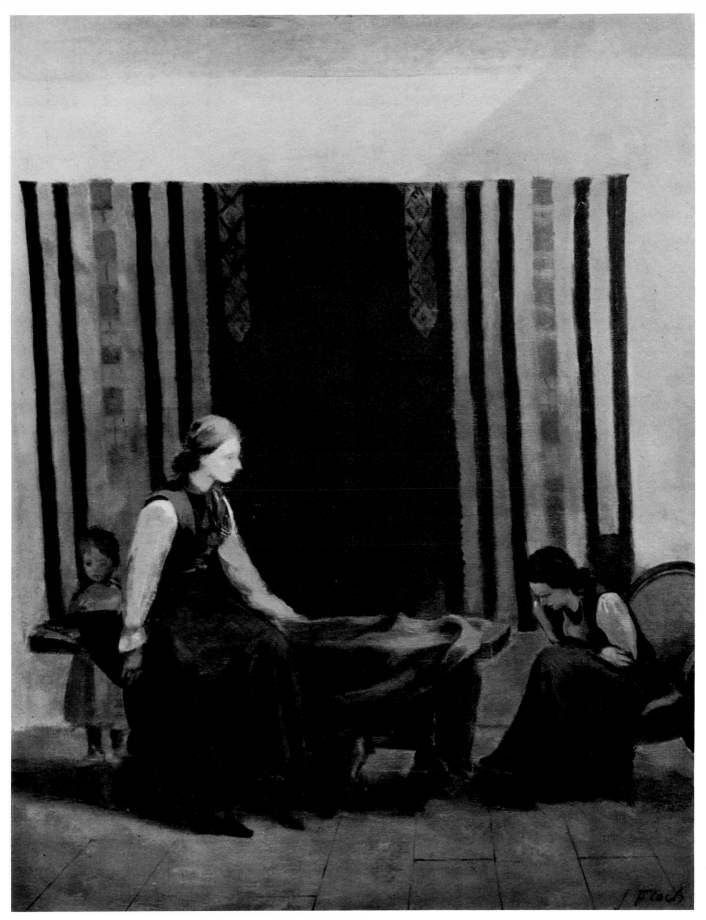

25 TAPESTRY

26 CONVERSATION 1

27 View from a Window

28 TERRACE WITH ROCK

29 WOMAN SEATED

30 TERASSE ANIMÉE

THE NEW WORLD

THE STUDIO

31 ROCKY LANDSCAPE

49

32 Silent Room

33 BRIDGE

34 MANHATTAN ROOFS

35 PENTHOUSE TERRACE

36 ROOFTOP IN MANHATTAN

37 CONSTRUCTION

38 MATERNITY

39 WOMAN

40 Interior with Black Screen

41 Sisters

42 FISHERMAN

43 STAIRWAY

44 Brooding Woman

45 BROWN SCREEN

46 STUDIO WITH SEASHELL

ON THE TERRACE

REST

47 GIRL

48 VIEW IN SAN FRANCISCO

49 Maternity

50 Head

51 WATERING THE FLOWERS

52 DOROTHY

53 THE FISHERBOAT

54 END OF DAY

55 Looking toward the City

56 THE CITY

57 FIGURE AND STILL LIFE, 1

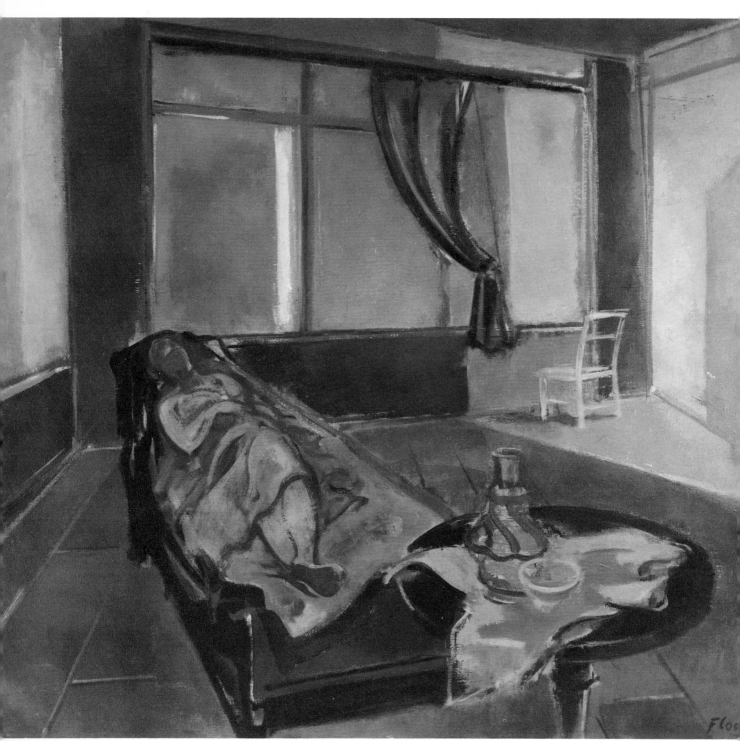

57A FIGURE AND STILL LIFE, 2

58 COMPOSITION

59 CYNTHIA

60 TERRACE

61 THE CURTAIN

Dog on Terrace

Rest

62 Mimi

63 TWO CHILDREN

64 Canal St. Martin

65 STILL LIFE WITH PITCHER

66 GREENHOUSE

67 END OF DAY

68 La Cité

69 VIEW THROUGH THE DOOR

70 BATHERS

71 TERRACE WITH STILLIFE

72 Model Resting

73 THE YELLOW DRESS

92

74 FIELDS

75 REST 2

76 WINTER

77 Looking toward the City

STANDING NUDE

The Island

78 INTERIOR WITH FLOWERS

79 IN THE STUDIO

80 YOUNG GIRL

81 DRAWING

82 THE CITY

83 IN MY STUDIO

102

84 THE MIRROR

85 THE ISLAND

86 SELF PORTRAIT

87 ROCKY LANDSCAPE

88 STILL LIFE WITH YELLOW BOTTLE

89 THE BLACK CHAIR

90 Evening

91 TWO ROADS

110

92 PORTOFINO

93 Sketch

Young Women

DUNES

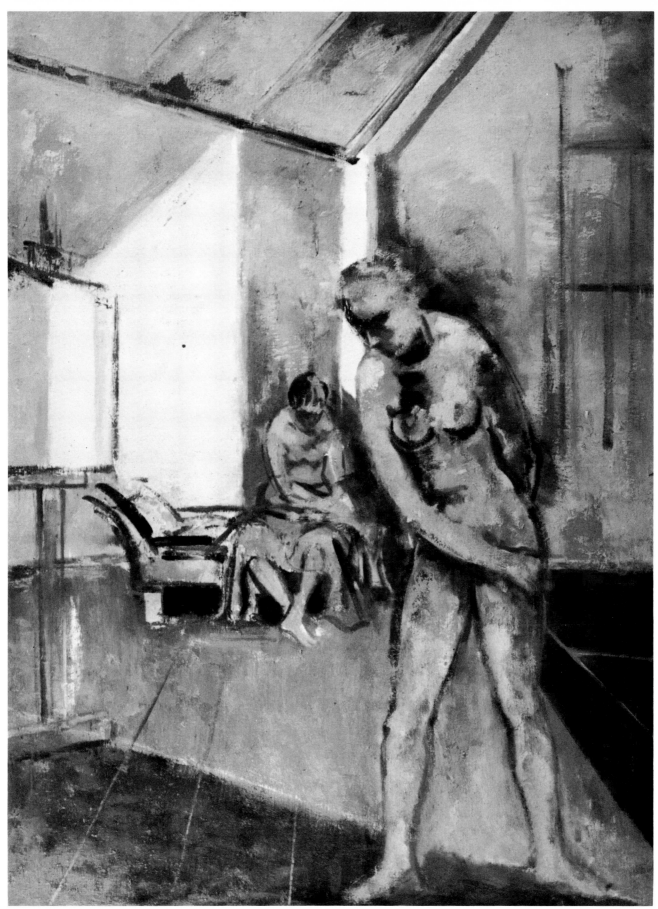

94 The Models

95 TWO WINDOWS

96 MAN WITH BIRD

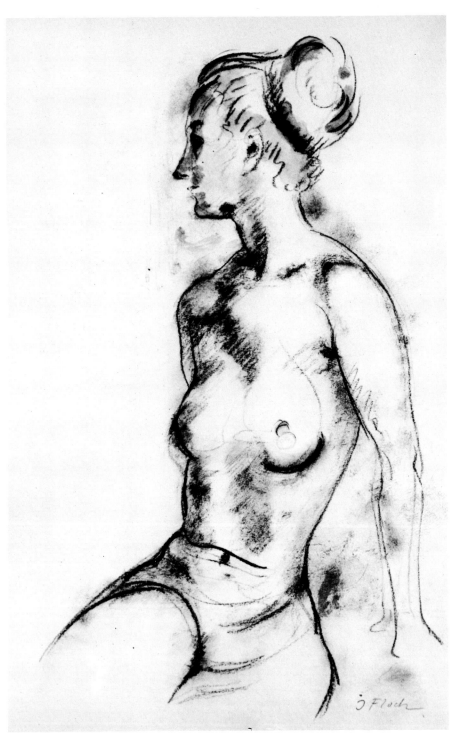

97 NUDE

116

98 WOMAN WALKING

1964

by Jacques Lipchitz
J. Floch

99 JACQUES LIPCHITZ

100 ISLAND IN GREECE

101 PAINTER & MODEL

102 Interior with two Figures

103 MAN, WASHDRAWING

104 SELF PORTRAIT

105 Seagulls

124

106 Conversation with Child

107 Afternoon

108 Chairs

109 Interior with Easel

110 Nude in Hallway

111 ARTIST AND HIS WIFE

112 Sculpture

113 Still Life with Pitcher

114 GREENHOUSE

115 DOORWAY

116 SEASHELL AND BOTTLES

117 Near the Sea

118 SILENT CORNER

119 Pause

120 Young Woman

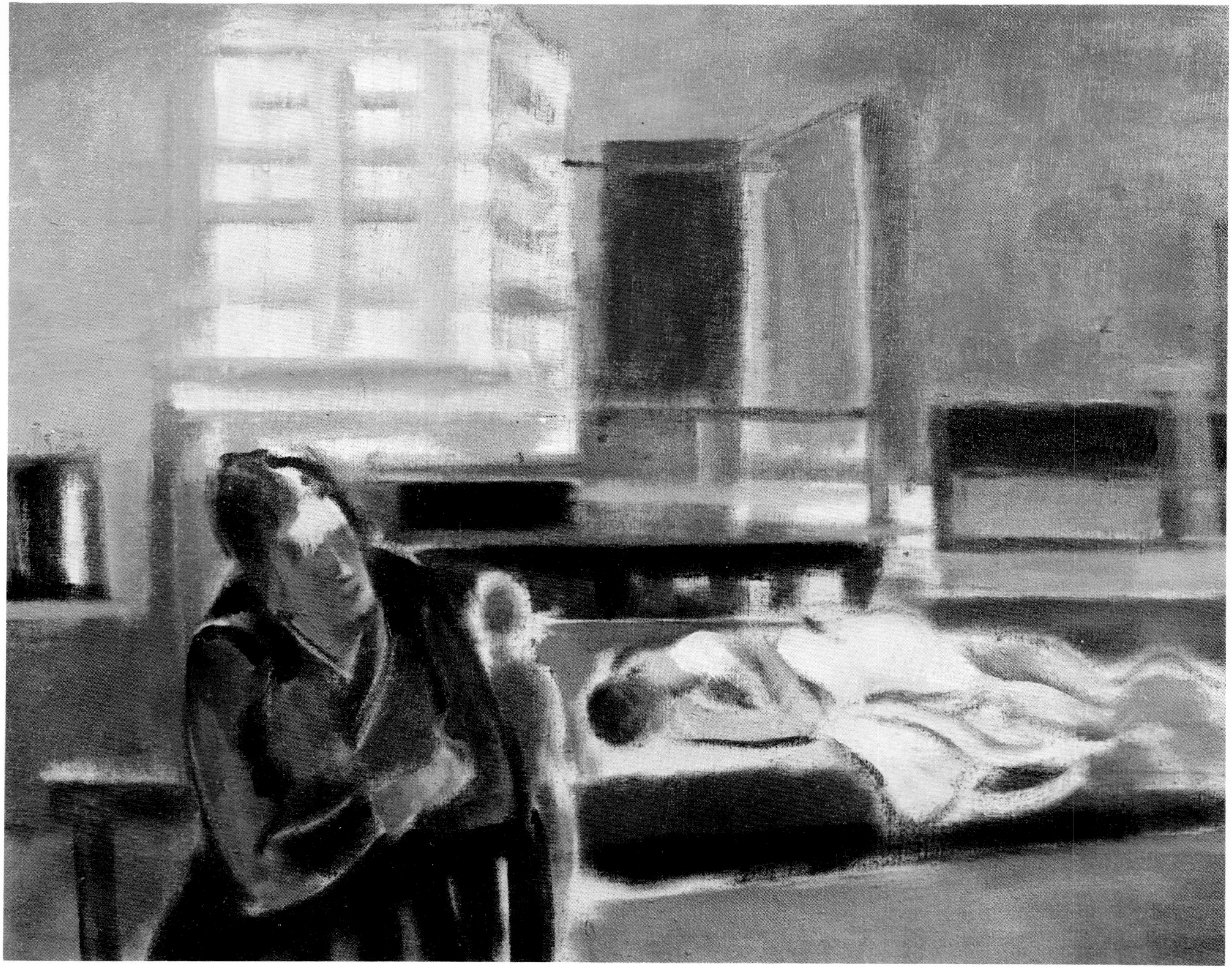

121 Evening on a Terrace

122 THE BLACK SCREEN

123 Woman with Flowers

124 Studio with Sculpture and Nude

143